2026 MINUTES

OF THE

CALLED MEETING

OF

GENERAL ASSEMBLY

CUMBERLAND PRESBYTERIAN CHURCH

January 23, 2026

Office of the General Assembly

Cumberland Presbyterian Church

February 2026

8207 Traditional Place
Cordova (Memphis), Tennessee 38016

Published and distributed by The Discipleship Ministry Team, CPC Memphis, Tennessee

The Discipleship Ministry Team of the Ministry Council of the Cumberland Presbyterian Church is the successor organization to the Board of Christian Education of the Cumberland Presbyterian Church.

Funded, in part, by your contributions to Our United Outreach.

First Edition 2026

ISBN: 978-1-945929-59-5

2026 MINUTES

of the
General Assembly
Cumberland Presbyterian Church

****

CALLED MEETING
BRENTWOOD, TENNESSEE
JANUARY 23, 2026

****

NEXT MEETING

JUNE-14-19, 2026
ROGERS, ARKANSAS

TABLE OF CONTENTS

Called Meeting of the General Assembly
January 23-24, 2026
Nashville, Tennessee

AGENDA

Assembly Meeting: Brenthaven Cumberland Presbyterian Church, Brentwood, Tennessee
Moderator: Rev. Jhony Montaño
Pastor Host: Rev. Kip Rush

FRIDAY, JANUARY 23, 2026

Time	Event
11:00am– 12:30pm	Registration for Commissioners and Youth Advisory Delegates
1:00 pm	Worship
1:30 pm	Call to Order Constituting Prayer Welcome, Moderator Welcome, Pastor Host Report of the Credentials Committee Statement of the Call Adoption of the Agenda
2:00pm	Presentations by MTS Board of Trustees and the Special GA Committee (15 minute recess following presentations)
3:15pm	Resume business for Informal Consideration of the reports (Q & A).
5:30 pm	Break for Dinner
7:00 pm	General Assembly Business
9:00 pm	Adjournment or recess until Saturday morning

(closing worship will be either Friday night or following business on Saturday morning)

SATURDAY, JANUARY 24, 2026

8:30am	General Assembly Business

COMMISSIONERS
to the
ONE HUNDRED NINETY-FOURTH GENERAL ASSEMBLY

PRESBYTERY	MINISTER	ELDER
Andes (1)	Luz Maria Heilbron	Andrea Mesa
Arkansas (2	Bobby Coleman	
Cauca Valley (4)	Fabian Florez	Mercedes del Real
	Johny Montano	Janneth Naranjo
Choctaw (1)	Mike Sharpe	
Columbia (1)	Jimmy Peyton	Brenda Howell
Cornerstone (5)	Rob Harris	Susan Fitzgerald
	Keith Harwell	David Long
	Mitch Boulton	Donald Moore
	Bill James	
Covenant (3)	Larry Buchanan	Laura DeHart
	Curtis Franklin	Mike Hardesty
	Marc Bell	Albert Russell
Cumberland (3)	Aaron Craig	Kathy Allen
Cumberland East Coast (1)		
Del Cristo (2)	Timothy Young	
East Tennessee (3)	Larry Blakeburn	Tony Bird
	Ronnie Duncan	
	Thomas Sweet	
Emaus (1)	Ana Cecilia Taborda	William Paez
Grace (3)	Daniel Barkley	
	Karen Linski	
	David Linski	
Hong Kong (2)		
Hope (1)		
Japan (2)		
Midsouth (1)	Mike Qualls	
Missouri (1)		Bruce Cook
Murfreesboro (3)	Kevin Twilla	
	Jeff Clark	Tim McDonald
	Lisa Oliver	
Nashville (3)	Jason Mikel	Elizabeth Mills
	Emri Rogers	Guin Tyus
	Kip Rush	
North Central (1)	Juan David Correa	
Red River (3)		
Robert Donnell (1)	Darren Kennemer	Mo Orringer
Tenn/Georgia (2)	Mark Craven	
	Phillip Layne	
Trinity (1)	Rusty Rustenhaven	Linda Trejo-Todd

<u>Note</u>: Colombian commissioners and Bobby Coleman (General Assembly Special Committee member) participated by Zoom

YOUTH ADVISORY DELEGATES
to the
ONE HUNDRED NINETY-FOURTH GENERAL ASSEMBLY
(Each Presbytery is eligible to send two Youth Advisory Delegates)

PRESBYTERY	DELEGATE
Arkansas	
Cauca Valley	
Choctaw	
Columbia	
Cornerstone	
Covenant	
Cumberland	
del Cristo	Esther Davis
East Tennessee	
Emaus	
Grace	
Hope	
Japan	
Midsouth	
Missouri	
Murfreesboro	
Nashville	
North Central	
Red River	
Robert Donnell	Ellie Kennemer
Tennessee Georgia	
Trinity	Daniel Rodriguez

THE REPORT OF THE BOARD OF TRUSTEES
OF MEMPHIS THEOLOGICAL SEMINARY (MTS)
JANUARY 23, 2026

A. Timeline of Strategic Planning and the MAP Process

This narrative provides a chronological overview of Memphis Theological Seminary's (MTS) strategic discernment process, culminating in the completion of its merger, acquisition, and partnership (MAP) evaluation. It reflects the Seminary's sustained commitment to institutional planning, financial stewardship, and mission integrity amid the evolving landscape of theological education. Each phase illustrates how the Seminary sought to ensure long-term sustainability while remaining faithful to its historic mission of forming Cumberland Presbyterians and other faith leaders in the way of Jesus.

June 2018

During the 2018 meeting of the General Assembly of the Cumberland Presbyterian Church, the Committee on Higher Education and the Children's Home recommended that the General Assembly establish an Evaluation Committee pertaining to Memphis Theological Seminary (MTS). A portion of the report reads: "…based on the recommendation adopted by the 2013 General Assembly for the creation of periodic Evaluation Committees to assess the entities and programs overseen by the Cumberland Presbyterian Church. The Committee recognizes and appreciates the mission and work of the Memphis Theological Seminary in preparing the future ministers and leaders of the Cumberland Presbyterian Church. We commend them on their efforts for diversity and relevance in our modern and ever-changing world. We express our concern over the financial deficits incurred by the Seminary over the last six years. We commend the Trustees for their decision to balance the budget within the next three years. We recognize that enrollment in the Seminary, and in Seminaries nationwide, is declining and endorse the measures taken by the Board of Trustees and the Faculty to increase the educational opportunities available to the student body of the Seminary. In recognition of the General Assembly's responsibility to maintain oversight of the Memphis Theological Seminary, and in partnership with them, the Committee makes the following recommendation to ensure that the General Assembly has the necessary information to effectively complete its oversight responsibilities."

June 4, 2018

The Association of Theological Schools (ATS) requested that Memphis Theological Seminary (MTS) submit, by November 1, 2019, a report demonstrating the development of a coherent and comprehensive institutional strategic plan focused on key priorities and including specific strategies for addressing the Seminary's major challenges.

December 2018

The Southern Association of Colleges and Schools Commission on Colleges (SACSCOC) Board denied MTS reaffirmation of accreditation, continued the Seminary's accreditation on warning for twelve months, and cited noncompliance with the following Core Requirements of the Principles of Accreditation: institutional planning; quality enhancement plan; student outcomes (educational programs); student support services staff; financial resources; financial documents; and financial responsibility.

October 28, 2019

MTS submitted its 2019–2023 Institutional Strategic Plan to ATS. The plan identified strategic priorities related to enrollment growth, financial sustainability, campus infrastructure, and academic excellence.

January 1, 2020

Jody Hill assumed the office of President of Memphis Theological Seminary. The Board of Trustees emphasized that strategic planning should remain an ongoing, institution-wide process. President Hill invited the leadership team, faculty, and broader seminary community into a renewed period of discernment and evaluation, building upon the framework of the 2019–2023 Strategic Plan.

March 2020

As with most institutions of higher education, MTS shifted its immediate focus to emergency management related to the COVID-19 pandemic, including the transition to online learning, financial stabilization, and support for students, faculty, and staff. Long-term strategic planning was temporarily deferred.

September 4, 2020

To resume strategic planning, President Hill began intensive meetings with the Planning and Evaluation (P&E) Committee of the Board of Trustees. Membership included Seminary administration, trustees, faculty representatives, Student Senate, denominational representatives, alumni, the Moderator of the Board, and external consultant Greg Henson, President of Kairos University. Mr. Henson facilitated discussions on sustainability and collaborative models emerging in theological education, including shared services, resource partnerships, and institutional mergers or acquisitions.

2021

Through the work of the P&E Committee and the Executive Leadership Team, MTS examined the changing landscape of theological education, including declining enrollment trends, shifts in denominational support, and rising operational costs. President Hill shared data compiled by Chris Meinzer of ATS highlighting the increasing number of seminary closures and mergers across North America. Meinzer's presentations—particularly Sustainability and Strategic Thinking and Leading Beyond the Blizzard—were instrumental in shaping MTS's awareness of sector-wide challenges and potential strategic responses.

2022

In fall 2022, the P&E Committee initiated a research-based evaluation of long-term sustainability options. The committee held six information-gathering meetings with Bethel University and Kairos University. Initial conversations assessed mission alignment, followed by exploration of financial sustainability options through partnership or collaboration.

October 7, 2022

At the fall Board meeting, President Hill presented ATS data demonstrating declining enrollment trends across North American theological institutions. He reported that MTS's operational model was not sustainable long-term and projected that the Seminary would require either an endowment increase of approximately $40 million or an annual revenue increase of $2 million to continue operating independently.

February 2023

Upon recommendation from the P&E Committee, the Board authorized the formal exploration of merger, acquisition, and partnership options as part of MTS's strategic planning process.

March 20, 2023

The P&E Committee met with Mike Sharpe, Stated Clerk and Chief Executive Officer of the Cumberland Presbyterian Church (CPC), to discuss the possibility of a covenant relationship that would relinquish CPC legal ownership of MTS, thereby allowing the Seminary greater autonomy to pursue strategic options while maintaining its historic denominational connection.

April 27, 2023

The P&E Committee met with Robert Heflin, Executive Director of the CPC Board of Stewardship, Foundation, and Benefits, to discuss implications for benefits, endowments, and fiduciary relationships should such a covenant relationship be adopted.

June 2023

MTS submitted its annual report to the General Assembly, analyzing ATS data to contextualize MTS within national trends. The report documented a decade-long enrollment decline consistent with peer institutions and introduced the need to generate approximately $2 million annually in new revenue or cost savings. Exploratory conversations with Bethel University and Kairos University ultimately proved nonviable due to accreditation hurdles, transition costs, and limited financial benefit.

Fall 2023

The Planning and Evaluation Committee concluded that long-term sustainability would require either merger or embeddedness with another institution. On October 5, 2023, Memphis Theological Seminary engaged Rebekah Basinger of the In Trust Center for Theological Schools as a strategic planning coach. On that date, she facilitated a retreat with faculty, staff, and trustees to guide discussion regarding the process and implications of a merger, acquisition, and partnership (MAP) evaluation.

On October 6, 2023, the Board of Trustees appointed a five-member exploratory committee to pursue formal conversations with potential MAP partners. With the conclusion of the 2019–2023 Institutional Strategic Plan, this work was designated as the Seminary's primary strategic planning focus.

June 2024

Memphis Theological Seminary submitted its annual report to the General Assembly of the Cumberland Presbyterian Church, informing the denomination that the Seminary was evaluating merger and partnership options for consideration by the 2024 General Assembly. The General Assembly acknowledged MTS's need to enter acquisition or merger discussions, expressed hope that initial conversations would begin with Bethel University, requested that all relevant Cumberland Presbyterian Church governing bodies be kept informed, and deferred any final action until additional information was available, including the possible need for a called meeting at an appropriate time.

Fall 2024

Through conversations with its accrediting bodies, the Association of Theological Schools (ATS) and the Southern Association of Colleges and Schools Commission on Colleges (SACSCOC), Memphis Theological Seminary learned that a merger with Bethel University would likely not receive SACSCOC consideration until June 2026 due to financial concerns at both institutions. As a result, formal merger negotiations were deferred.

November 2024

At the Board's direction, Seminary leadership initiated outreach to other financially stable, mission-aligned institutions, evaluating approximately thirty potential partners. It became increasingly clear that MTS's legal status as a CPC entity impeded negotiations, as uncertainty remained regarding which assets could be made available.

April 16, 2025

MTS submitted a report requesting that the General Assembly consider a Covenant Relationship model to facilitate further strategic options.

June 2025

The General Assembly declined the Covenant model and instead appointed a five-person General Assembly Special Committee on MTS. The Special Committee and the MTS Planning and Evaluation Committee met jointly on July 24, 2025 and agreed that operations could not continue beyond July 31, 2026 under the forecasted budget. Continuing operations would require an additional endowment draw of approximately $1 million beyond the standard 5 percent annual distribution. That additional draw would not be possible because endowment principal cannot be spent.

November 12–13, 2025

MTS met with the ATS Accreditation Evaluation Committee, which subsequently recommended reaffirmation of accreditation on probation due to noncompliance with Standard 10.3 (Financial Resources). If affirmed, MTS would be required to submit a teach-out agreement by April 15, 2026.

November 17, 2025

MTS President Jody Hill contacted Bethel University President Perry Moulds to inquire whether Bethel might be interested in submitting an acquisition proposal for consideration at the SACSCOC June 2026 meeting. President Moulds graciously responded that Bethel could not pursue an acquisition while MTS remains under its current ATS probationary status.

December 11, 2025

A called meeting of the Board of Trustees of Memphis Theological Seminary was held via Zoom to receive the final report of the Planning and Evaluation Committee following completion of the strategic discernment process.

Bobby Coleman of the General Assembly Special Committee on Memphis Theological Seminary (CP GA Special Committee) was also present for the Called Meeting. This report was crafted through transparent dialogue while seeking the full support of the CP GA Special Committee. We applaud the collegial spirit and partnership we have shared with the CP GA Special Committee in our effort to find common ground to serve the future of Cumberland Presbyterian theological education and to honor the historic and transformational ecumenical mission the CP Church created at Memphis Theological Seminary.

It was reported that thirty schools, denominations, or organizations were evaluated and/or contacted regarding possible merger, acquisition, or partnership.

Formal proposals were received from two institutions.

LeMoyne-Owen College offered to acquire Memphis Theological Seminary from the Cumberland Presbyterian Church and requested approximately $7.5 million (one-half) of

MTS endowments to support its transition into theological education and to maintain the current MTS tuition rate of $640 per credit hour.

Perkins School of Theology at Southern Methodist University submitted a comprehensive teach-out proposal to ensure that all current MTS students can complete their course of study should Memphis Theological Seminary close on July 31, 2026.

Under the Perkins proposal, all current MTS students would receive a 100 percent tuition scholarship. The estimated cost to Perkins is approximately $3 million. To replenish these scholarship funds, Perkins requested $3 million in non-CPC endowments, including approximately $2.1 million designated for Methodist students, $490,000 designated for African American students, $260,000 designated for PC(USA) students, and $150,000 designated as non-denominational funds.

Students would continue with the same remote or online learning opportunities currently available at MTS, with approximately one week per year of in-person instruction. Perkins committed to offering these in-person courses in Memphis, maintaining a Memphis presence, and enrolling new students in the area beginning Fall 2026.

Perkins committed to hiring one MTS faculty member, Dr. Farris Blount. No other MTS faculty or staff will be retained. For doctoral programs, Perkins committed to continuing to utilize current MTS adjunct faculty to ensure continuity for doctoral students.

The Perkins proposal is time-sensitive and must be executed no later than January 31, 2026, allowing MTS to notify students by that date. Students would have until March 31, 2026 to decide whether to transfer to Perkins for Fall 2026 enrollment.

Accrediting agencies have approved the Perkins teach-out framework to ensure the transferability of all coursework. MTS will also work to assist students who choose to transfer to institutions other than Perkins.

If MTS ceases official operations on July 31, 2026, approximately twelve employees will remain employed through no later than December 31, 2026, to continue campus maintenance and safety functions and to complete legal, financial, accreditation, and other operational wind-down responsibilities.

MTS may make an additional draw of approximately $500,000 from unrestricted endowment funds, beyond the approved July 31, 2026 budget, to support final operations, including retention and severance costs. No donor-restricted endowment principal or corpus will be used; the additional draw would be funded exclusively from investment earnings.

A motion was made and seconded to accept the Perkins School of Theology proposal and recommend this course of action to the Cumberland Presbyterian Church General Assembly.

The motion carried without a negative vote.

Trustees present for the vote were Mike Allen, Daniel Barkley, Jill Bryant, Tyrone Burroughs, Gloria Diaz, Wes Johnson, Rose Mary Magrill, Lisanne Marshall, Vanessa Midgett, Jimmy Mosby, Susan Parker, Kip Rush, and Hilary Dow Ward

B. Recommendation to the General Assembly of the Cumberland Presbyterian Church

Recommendation:
That the General Assembly approve the closure of Memphis Theological Seminary effective July 31, 2026, and authorize the Seminary to proceed with a formal teach-out plan in partnership with Perkins School of Theology at Southern Methodist University.

This recommendation is offered with deep gratitude for the Seminary's sixty-year ministry, profound concern for its students and employees, and unwavering commitment to theological education in service to the Cumberland Presbyterian Church and the wider body of Christ.

Respectfully submitted,
Kip Rush, Moderator of th Board of Trustees
Jody Hill, President

THE REPORT OF THE GENERAL ASSEMBLY SPECIAL COMMITTEE ON MEMPHIS THEOLOGICAL SEMINARY AND CLERGY/LEADERSHIP TRAINING

This General Assembly Special Committee (referred to below as "the Committee") makes the following report and recommendations to the General Assembly at its special called meeting held January 23-24, 2026, at Brenthaven Cumberland Presbyterian Church, Brentwood, Tennessee.

EXECUTIVE SUMMARY

The bullet-points summarize the matters addressed in this Report:

• The Committee supports the decision of the Board of Trustees of Memphis Theological Seminary to cease teaching operations as of July 31, 2026.

• While fully supporting the decision of the MTS Board, the Committee offers a recommendation that differs slightly from the Recommendation in the MTS Report.

• The Program of Alternate Studies (PAS) will continue while MTS winds down its operations and after MTS ceases operations.

• It is in the best interests of the Cumberland Presbyterian Church for the General Assembly to act in a manner which respects the legal structures of the denomination and the shared governance relationship between the General Assembly and MTS.

• The Committee is recommending the organization of a new Cumberland Presbyterian entity to house the Program of Alternate Studies and to help promote and support theological education for ministers and lay leaders.

• The Committee would like Memphis Theological Seminary, as an interim measure, to use MTS endowment funds, as permitted by law, to provide and administer appropriate scholarships for the theological education of Cumberland Presbyterians.

• The Committee believes it is in the best interests of the Cumberland Presbyterian Church for MTS to list its Memphis campus for sale, subject to the right of the General Assembly Corporation to approve any sale.

• The board of directors of the General Assembly Corporation, upon the recommendation of this Committee, should be authorized to act on behalf of the General Assembly Corporation in matters relating to winding down the Memphis Theological Seminary corporation.

I. FORMATION OF THE COMMITTEE

The 194th General Assembly of the Cumberland Presbyterian Church, meeting in Knoxville, Tennessee, adopted the following recommendations in the report of the Higher Education/Cumberland Youth and Family Services Committee:

RECOMMENDATION 6: That the 194th General Assembly appoint a special committee with Jaime Jordan as legal advisor, to work in conjunction with the Memphis Theological Seminary in Merger, Affiliation, and Partnership discussions, to review and evaluate all options and determine future needs for Clergy/Leadership Training in the denomination, in consultation with the General Assembly Corporation, the Pastoral Development Ministry Team, and the Program of Alternate Studies.

RECOMMENDATION 7: That the Moderator appoint the following persons to be members of the committee formed by Recommendation 6: Rev. Dr. Larry Blakeburn (East Tennessee), Elder Dr. Mo Ottinger (Robert Donnell), Rev. Bobby Coleman (Arkansas), Rev. David Linski (Grace), Rev. Lisa Oliver (Murfreesboro).

II. BACKGROUND

The Committee determined the following to be its primary duties:
1. To study any proposals which Memphis Theological Seminary might receive for a merger, affiliation, or partnership from a third party.

2. To represent the interests of the General Assembly and be prepared to discuss with MTS any changes that might be desirable in order for the Committee to recommend a merger, affiliation, or partnership proposal to the General Assembly.

3. To consider options for continuing training for Cumberland Presbyterian clergy and leadership in the event Memphis Theological Seminary should find it necessary to discontinue its educational operations.

4. To report back to the General Assembly such information and recommendations as it deemed necessary.

The Committee has met several times, with Rev. Michael Sharpe (Stated Clerk) and Mr. Jaime Jordan (legal counsel) present for each meeting. The Committee held one or more meetings with Reverend Dr. Jody Hill (President of Memphis Theological Seminary); representatives of the Board of Trustees of Memphis Theological Seminary; Reverend Dr. Michael Qualls (Director Cumberland Presbyterian House of Studies, Director Program of Alternate Studies and Vice-President for Cumberland Presbyterian Church Relations); Mr. Robert Heflin and Reverend Brittany Meeks (executive staff of the Board of Stewardship, Foundation, and Benefits); and, representing the Ministry Council, Reverend Dr. Pam Phillips-Burk (Pastoral Development Ministry Team Leader), Reverend Dr. Milton Ortiz (Missions Ministry Team Leader), and Reverend Jen Newell (Program Director of the Louisa Woosley Preaching Initiative).

The Committee expresses its deep appreciation to all of these individuals for their help, support, insights, and prayers. The Committee would like to particularly thank Rev. Dr. Jody Hill and Rev. Kip Rush, chair of the Board of Trustees of Memphis Theological Seminary, for their extraordinary openness and cooperation.

III. SHARED GOVERNANCE OF MEMPHIS THEOLOGICAL SEMINARY

The Cumberland Presbyterian Church has organized itself in a corporate form for conducting business. Two of the corporations in the Cumberland Presbyterian Church legal structure are the Cumberland Presbyterian Church General Assembly Corporation ("CPCGAC") and Memphis Theological Seminary of the Cumberland Presbyterian Church (MTS). Both are nonprofit corporations organized under Tennessee laws that govern nonprofit, religious corporations.

Tennessee nonprofit corporations are allowed to have "members" as that term is defined by state law. MTS has a single member, that being the CPCGAC. The Board of MTS and the CPCGAC share governance of MTS in very specific ways prescribed by law:

• As a separate corporation, MTS is governed by its Board of Trustees and corporate officers who are elected by the Board or selected by the President. The MTS Board is solely responsible for the operations of MTS and is charged with establishing policies for the MTS corporation, electing its President, and taking responsibility for the management and day-to-day operations of the corporation. In short, the MTS Board exercises all rights with respect to MTS except for certain enumerated rights which are reserved to its sole member (CPCGAC) by state law or by the MTS corporate charter.

• Under this system of shared governance, the MTS Board operates the MTS corporation, and the CPCGAC enjoys the following specific rights:

  • MTS cannot merge with another corporation without the prior written consent of the CPCGAC.

  • MTS cannot dissolve without the prior written consent of the CPCGAC.

• MTS cannot sell, lease, exchange, or otherwise dispose of all, or substantially all, of its property without the prior written consent of the CPCGAC.

• MTS cannot amend its corporate charter without the prior written consent of the CPCGAC.

• Only the CPCGAC can elect or remove a trustee of MTS

• In the event MTS is dissolved, the remaining assets of the corporation must be distributed to the CPCGAC.

Tennessee law grants a special immunity to a member of a nonprofit corporation:

48-56-203. Member's liability to third parties.
A member of a corporation is not, as such, personally liable for the acts, debts, liabilities, or obligations of the corporation.

This means that a member is generally not liable for a corporation's acts, debts, liabilities, or obligations just because of the member-corporation relationship. However, if a member engages in certain conduct with respect to the corporation, particularly conduct outside the scope of a member's rights, then the member can be liable for the corporation's acts, debts, liabilities, or obligations.

Under Tennessee law, this shifting of one corporation's obligations to that corporation's parent body can occur when the parent ignores the legal distinction between the member and the corporation and "exercises complete dominion over its subsidiary, not only of finances, but of policy and business practice in respect to the transaction under attack, so that the corporate entity, as to that transaction, had no separate mind, will, or existence of its own." (Legal citation omitted)

In order to avoid creating or supporting an argument that the CPCGAC should be held liable for any debts, obligations, or liabilities of MTS, the Committee urges the General Assembly to respect the boundaries of its shared governance of MTS. The Committee recommends that the CPCGAC take special care to "play only its side of the net" when dealing with the MTS report and this Committee report.

IV. COMMENTS AND RECOMMENDATIONS ON THE REPORT OF MTS

The MTS Report to the General Assembly is detailed. It explains the efforts of the MTS Board and President Hill to find a way for the Seminary to continue its educational mission. Unfortunately, MTS has concluded that continuing to operate its educational program has been made impractical by rising costs, decreasing enrollment, and a limited endowment.

The Committee has not attempted to independently confirm the financial conclusions described in the MTS Report nor all of the actions by MTS to avoid closure. The Committee is mindful that such areas are the province of MTS and its Board. However, MTS has generously shared information and answered the Committee's questions throughout this process.

One of the primary functions of the Committee – that being to work in conjunction with MTS in Merger, Affiliation, and Partnership discussions – has been rendered moot. At present there is no offer from any seminary, university, or denomination to engage in a merger, partnership, or acquisition with MTS.

The Committee expresses the following opinions with respect to the MTS Report:

1. The information in the MTS report is accurate to the best of the Committee's knowledge.

2. MTS has made commendable efforts to find a way to keep MTS operating. Unfortunately, those efforts have been unproductive.

3. MTS is prepared to turn its attention to winding up the Seminary's operations in a responsible manner. MTS has expressed to the Committee a commitment to help the students of MTS complete their theological educations and to provide modest financial incentives to reward MTS employee who remain employed at MTS until operations can be brought to a systematic close.

4. MTS is in the process of making arrangements for the "teach-out" of those MTS students who will still need to complete their educational degrees after the Seminary's proposed date to close its teaching programs. An approved teach-out plan is required by the State of Tennessee and the Seminary's accrediting bodies. Although establishing a proper teach-out plan with Perkins School of Theology at Southern Methodist University is within the responsibility of the MTS Board rather than with the CPCGAC, the Committee accepts the MTS Board's decision that the proposed plan with Perkins is in the best interests of MTS and its students.

The MTS Report contains a single recommendation from its Board of Trustees:

That the General Assembly approve the closure of Memphis Theological Seminary effective July 31, 2026, and authorize the Seminary to proceed with a formal teach-out plan in partnership with Perkins School of Theology at Southern Methodist University.

The Committee is grateful that the MTS Board has chosen not to take these dire actions without seeking a consensus with the CPCGAC. At the same time, the Committee considers it important for the CPCGAC to express its support for the plan presented by the MTS Board in a manner which acknowledges the respective roles of the MTS Board and the CPCGAC. Accordingly, the Committee makes the following recommendation:

RECOMMENDATION 1: That the Recommendation in section B of the Report of the Board of Trustees of Memphis Theological Seminary, which reads as follows:

That the General Assembly approve the closure of Memphis Theological Seminary effective July 31, 2026, and authorize the Seminary to proceed with a formal teach-out plan in partnership with Perkins School of Theology at Southern Methodist University.

be denied, and that the following recommendation be adopted in its stead:

That the General Assembly express its deep sadness at the need to discontinue the educational mission of Memphis Theological Seminary and express thanks to God for the Seminary's long history of preparing and educating ministers of the gospel; and
That the General Assembly express its appreciation for the hard work of the MTS Board of Trustees and its support for the difficult decision of the Board to cease classroom operations as of July 31, 2026, in light of current economic realities; and
That the General Assembly express its support of MTS's intention to enter into an appropriate, formal teach-out plan with Perkins School of Theology at Southern Methodist University.

V. FUTURE EFFORTS TO ADVANCE THEOLOGICAL EDUCATION IN THE CUMBERLAND PRESBYTERIAN CHURCH

The Committee spent a significant amount of time discussing how best to meet the needs of the Cumberland Presbyterian Church to educate clergy and lay leaders in a post-MTS era. As a result of these discussions, including critical input from leaders of the Pastoral Development Ministry Team and the Program of Alternate Studies, the Committee is recommending that the General Assembly approve in principle the creation of a new denominational entity. For convenience, the Committee called this new entity the Committee on Theological Education (or "COTE"), although the name is subject to change.

COTE is still in the planning stages, and there is much work to be done in order to complete the vision of how COTE can best meet the denomination's needs. In broad strokes, the Committee believes that COTE would carry out the following ministries:

A. Oversee a Theological School Education Fund. COTE would manage permanent endowments currently managed by MTS or the Board of Stewardship and use the proceeds from the funds to provide scholarship and other support for CP students pursuing theological education at an accredited school. The fund could also be used to support other types of education and training for CP ministers, church educators, church professionals, and lay ministry.

B. Maintain the Program of Alternate Studies. Over and over the Committee was asked, "Will PAS survive the closing of MTS?" and "How can we make PAS stronger?" While the Committee believes that formal seminary training remains critical to our denomination, it also recognizes that a strong PAS program will be more important than ever in a post-MTS era.

COTE would be responsible for operating a revitalized PAS program with the goal of increasing its multi-cultural global reach and providing more robust offerings. For example, the Committee would like to see PAS develop a more user-friendly, learn-at-your-own-pace curriculum and supplement the PAS curriculum with seminary course work.

C. Provide more training for lay leadership. COTE would take action to enhance the lay leadership track currently available through PAS or identify and utilize programs similar to those in place at other seminaries. The lay leadership curriculum could be supplemented with Cumberland Presbyterian adjunct Instructors for denominational specific courses such as: Cumberland Presbyterian History, Theology, Polity and Ministerial Formation.

D. Oversee the Cumberland Presbyterian House of Studies and Cumberland Presbyterian Formation Groups. COTE would be a resource to Presbyteries and to CP students pursuing a seminary education, PAS certification, or Lay Ministry certification. COTE would work to ensure that those CP students who are enrolled in a particular seminary OR certified Lay Ministry Program are formed in the distinct ethos of the Reformed and Cumberland Presbyterian theological tradition. For example, COTE might help sponsor denominational courses (eg, CP History, Theology and Polity) at one or more seminaries, connecting seminary students with presbyteries for services and support. COTE could provide denominational information to students, including scholarship and service loan opportunities.

Again, more work is needed to flesh out the practical aspects of COTE. Some of the key questions to be answered are:

• How will COTE be constituted? The Committee discussed the possibility of nine (9) members elected by the General Assembly along with ex officio members who might be General Assembly staff, Board of Stewardship staff, or members of the Pastoral Development Ministry Team of the Ministry Council. COTE could also include guest representatives from approved theological institutions.

• How will COTE be staffed? Initial staff could include a COTE Coordinator, PAS Director, Lay Ministry Director, CP House of Studies Director, and support staff.

• How will COTE be funded? The Committee hopes that COTE could be funded through a combination of available MTS endowments for operations, the current allocations for MTS and PAS through Our United Outreach, or proceeds from the sale of the MTS campus. At present, there is likely sufficient space at the Cumberland Presbyterian Denominational Center to house COTE.

The Committee hopes to be ready to present a concrete recommendation for creating COTE to the 195th General Assembly in June, 2026. In order to do that, the Committee is asking for more time to consult with trustees and staff of MTS and for the appointment of two (2) additional members with appropriate expertise. The Committee is suggesting that it nominate persons to Moderator Jhony Montaño for his appointment.

RECOMMENDATION 2: That the General Assembly authorize the special committee created by the 194th General Assembly to continue working on the concept of a denominational entity that would house the Program of Alternate Studies and help to promote and support theological education for ministers and lay leaders; and

That the special committee nominate two new members for the special committee, with such new members subject to appointment by Moderator Jhony Montaño.

VI. ACTIONS WITH RESPECT TO MEMPHIS THEOLOGICAL SEMINARY

The Committee is of the opinion that the General Assembly needs to take action with respect to several issues related to Memphis Theological Seminary. These issues are addressed below.

A. Encouraging MTS to administer existing scholarship funds as a means of continuing its mission of religious education in the short term until a new denominational entity can be created.

It may be some months before a new denominational entity can fill the role of COTE described in Section V of this Report. In the meantime, the Cumberland Presbyterian Church should encourage and financially support the education of candidates seeking to become ministers in Cumberland Presbyterian churches.

The Committee believes that MTS would be the best choice for an entity to fill this need in the short term. MTS has access to endowments funds as well as the experience and expertise to award and administer scholarships to Cumberland Presbyterians who are seeking to further their theological education.

While the Committee believes it is beyond the scope of the CPCGAC's authority to direct the MTS corporation to undertake this task, it would be appropriate to request and encourage MTS to continue administering scholarships for theological education.

RECOMMENDATION 3: That the General Assembly respectfully request and encourage Memphis Theological Seminary to use MTS endowment funds, as permitted by law, to provide and administer appropriate scholarships for theological education to ministerial candidates under the care of a presbytery of the Cumberland Presbyterian Church.

B. Assisting MTS with the sale or other disposition of its campus.

The corporate charter of MTS provides that MTS cannot "sell, lease, exchange, or otherwise dispose of all, or substantially all, of its property" without the prior written consent of the CPCGAC. The Committee believes that it is in the best interests of the CPCGAC that the campus of MTS be sold and that the property be listed for sale as soon as possible.

There are several reasons why the Committee recommends that a sale of the campus move forward as quickly as possible. Real estate professionals have suggested that it could easily take a year or longer to close a sale of the campus. In the meantime there would be issues and expenses related to maintenance, security, and insurance. When the property is no longer being used for a religious and educational purposes, state law requires the property to be placed back on the tax rolls and property taxes assessed. The sale of the property for development is complicated by zoning and other legal issues.

Although the Committee believes it is entirely premature for the CPCGAC to approve any sale, lease, or disposal of the campus, the Committee believes it would serve the best interests of the Cumberland Presbyterian Church to request and encourage MTS to begin the process of selling the campus, with the understanding that formal approval of a sale would occur when an acceptable offer has been secured.

RECOMMENDATION 4: That the General Assembly respectfully request and encourage Memphis Theological Seminary to pursue the sale or other disposition of the Memphis campus and its contents as soon as practical, subject to the right of the Cumberland Presbyterian Church General Assembly Corporation to consent in writing to any sale or disposition of substantially all of the assets of Memphis Theological Seminary.

C. The General Assembly Corporation needs an expedited means of exercising its corporate rights in relation to the termination of the MTS corporation

The Committee has discussed that there are several decisions relating to the termination of the operations of MTS that may or will require the participation of MTS. In some cases, these decisions may be driven by legal concerns. In other cases, it may simply be a matter of the General Assembly exercising its financial judgment or encouraging MTS to take certain actions that the General Assembly believes to be in the best interests of the Cumberland Presbyterian Church.

Examples of these issues include:
• Should CPCGAC consent to the dissolution of the MTS corporation?
• If so, when should that dissolution occur in order to serve the best interests of the Cumberland Presbyterian Church?
• Should the CPCGAC consent to the merger of the MTS corporation into another Cumberland Presbyterian entity?
• If a merger is in the best interests of the Cumberland Presbyterian Church, when should that merger occur and who should be the parties to that merger?

• Should a specific offer to purchase substantially all of the assets of MTS be approved by the CPCGAC, and should that approval require the delay and expense of a called meeting of the General Assembly?
• Who can provide written consent if the Cumberland Presbyterian Church is required to give its consent to a court or regulatory body before MTS endowment funds can be used for purposes which have been approved by the General Assembly (such as the teach-out plan)?

The Committee is of the opinion that it would be impractical and unwise for all of these decisions to require a meeting of the General Assembly. The Committee believes that the commissioners should vest in the board of directors of the CPCGAC the authority to make appropriate and necessary decisions relating to the winding up of its affairs by MTS. Because such a grant of authority is unusual and because the Committee has spent significant time becoming acquainted with the issues and the consequences of various decisions, the Committee suggests that the CPCGAC board of directors act only in accordance with a recommendation by the Committee.

In other words, the CPCGAC board of directors could act without a special meeting of General Assembly, but both the CPCGAC and the Committee would have to agree before a corporate action relating to the termination of the affairs of MTS could occur. This would allow the CPCGAC to act quickly and efficiently but only if the board of directors and the Committee are in accord.

This plan would basically double the number of persons who must form a consensus in order for an action to be taken in the name of the General Assembly. If the board of directors and the Committee cannot agree, then the option to hold a special meeting of General Assembly is available.

RECOMMENDATION 5: That the General Assembly authorize its board of directors to exercise any and all of the corporate powers of the General Assembly Corporation in matters related to the winding down of operations of Memphis Theological Seminary, including but not limited to matters such as its dissolution, its merger, the disposition of substantially all of its assets, and the transfer of endowments in connection with its approved teach-out plan; provided, however, that the board of directors shall exercise these powers only upon the recommendation of the special committee created by the 194th General Assembly.

SUMMARY OF RECOMMENDATIONS

The five (5) recommendations of the Committee contained in this report are listed below for convenient reference:

RECOMMENDATION 1: That the Recommendation in section B of the Report of the Board of Trustees of Memphis Theological Seminary, which reads as follows:

That the General Assembly approve the closure of Memphis Theological Seminary effective July 31, 2026, and authorize the Seminary to proceed with a formal teach-out plan in partnership with Perkins School of Theology at Southern Methodist University.

be denied, and that the following recommendation be adopted in its stead:

That the General Assembly express its deep sadness at the need to discontinue the educational mission of Memphis Theological Seminary and express appreciation to God for the Seminary's long history of preparing and educating ministers of the gospel; and
That the General Assembly express its appreciation for the hard work of the MTS Board of Trustees and its support for the difficult decision of the Board to cease classroom operations as of July 31, 2026, in light of current economic realities; and
That the General Assembly express its support of MTS's intention to enter into an appropriate, formal teach-out plan with Perkins School of Theology at Southern Methodist University.

RECOMMENDATION 2: That the General Assembly authorize the special committee created by the 194th General Assembly to continue working on the concept of a denominational entity that would house the Program of Alternate Studies and help to promote and support theological education for ministers and lay leaders; and
That the special committee nominate two new members for the special committee, with such new members subject to appointment by Moderator Jhony Montaño.

RECOMMENDATION 3: That the General Assembly respectfully request and encourage Memphis Theological Seminary to use MTS endowment funds, as permitted by law, to provide and administer appropriate scholarships for theological education to ministerial candidates under the care of a presbytery of the Cumberland Presbyterian Church.

RECOMMENDATION 4: That the General Assembly respectfully request and encourage Memphis Theological Seminary to pursue the sale or other disposition of the Memphis campus and its contents as soon as practical, subject to the right of the Cumberland Presbyterian Church General Assembly Corporation to consent in writing to any sale or disposition of substantially all of the assets of Memphis Theological Seminary.

RECOMMENDATION 5: That the General Assembly authorize its board of directors to exercise any and all of the corporate powers of the General Assembly Corporation in matters related to the winding down of operations of Memphis Theological Seminary, including but not limited to matters such as its dissolution, its merger, the disposition of substantially all of its assets, and the transfer of endowments in connection with its approved teach-out plan; provided, however, that the board of directors shall exercise these powers only upon the recommendation of the special committee created by the 194th General Assembly.

The
Proceedings
of the

CALLED MEETING

of the

GENERAL ASSEMBLY

of the

CUMBERLAND PRESBYTERIAN CHURCH

session held in

BRENTHAVEN CUMBERLAND PRESBYTERIAN CHURCH
BRENTWOOD, TENNESSEE

on
JANUARY 23, 2026

At Brentwood, Tennessee, and within the facilities of the Brenthaven Cumberland Presbyterian Church, there the twenty-third day of January in the year of our Lord, Two Thousand Twenty-Six, at the appointed hour of one o'clock in the afternoon, ministers and elder commissioners from the various presbyteries, youth advisory delegates, and visitors assembled in a called session.

WORSHIP

The General Assembly and visitors shared in worship. The Assembly Worship Director, the Reverend Jen Newell, Program Director for the Louisa Woosley Preaching Initiative presided in worship assisted by Linda Pulley, Pianist, Brenthaven Cumberland Presbyterian Church. Congregational hymns included "The Church's One Foundation" and "Great Is Thy Faithfulness." "Amazing Grace" was the special music. Newell read Ephesians 4:1-6, as the call to worship. Various Cumberland Presbyterians participated in a video quoting Ecclesiastes 3:1-8. Reverend Newell delivered a devotional entitled, "Tis the Season."

CALL TO ORDER

The Moderator, the Reverend Jhony Montaño, Cauca Valley Presbytery, called the Assembly to order at 1:40 p.m. He was assisted with translation by Jonathan Calheiros and David Montoya.

CONSTITUTING PRAYER

The Reverend Juan David Correo, North Central Presbytery, gave the Constituting Prayer.

WELCOME -- MODERATOR

The Moderator, the Reverend Jhony Montaño welcomed the Assembly and expressed appreciation to the Worship Director, the Reverend Jen Newell, and the worship participants for the worship.

WELCOME – HOST PASTOR

The Pastor Host, the Reverend Kip Rush, Nashville Presbytery, welcomed the Assembly and made necessary announcements.

STATED CLERK ANNOUNCEMENTS

The Reverend Michael Sharpe, Stated Clerk made announcements of interest to the Commissioners regarding the agenda. He asked that commissioners to be seated in the two center sections of the sanctuary. He spoke about the agenda and the parliamentary flexibility inherent in the time set aside for questions and answers.

REPORT OF THE ENGROSSING CLERK

Reverend Lisa A. Scott, Engrossing Clerk presented enrollment of Commissioners/ Delegates and Youth Advisory Delegates noting the changes in commissioners and an enrollment of thirty-four (34) ministers, nineteen (19) elders for a total of fifty-three (53) Commissioners/ Delegates and four (4) Youth Advisory Delegates as of 1:00 p.m.

STATEMENT OF THE CALL

The Statement of the Call (Appendix A) is found on page 31 of the 2026 Preliminary Minutes. It is briefly stated: to hear relevant reports and take appropriate actions with respect to Memphis Theological Seminary of the Cumberland Presbyterian Church and theological education.

ADOPTION OF THE AGENDA

A motion was made with second to adopt the agenda. On unanimous voice vote the General Assembly adopted the agenda.

PRESENTATIONS BY MEMPHIS THEOLOGICAL SEMINARY BOARD OF TRUSTEES AND GENERAL ASSEMBLY SPECIAL COMMITTEE ON MEMPHIS THEOLOGICAL SEMINARY AND CLERGY/LEADERSHIP TRAINING

Reverend Dr. Michael Qualls, Director of the Program of Alternate Studies made opening remarks, charting the history of Memphis Theological Seminary (MTS) while inviting listeners to consider the past contributions of the Seminary and the ways in which the institution has since its inception in 1956 blessed ministers and congregations throughout the Denomination. He encouraged those present by reading Isaiah 58:9-11.

Reverend Dr. Jody Hill, President of MTS acknowledged the important role of Reverend Qualls as Vice-President of Cumberland Presbyterian Church Relations. He then went on to introduce MTS Board of Trustee Chair, the Reverend Kip Rush, the Reverend Daniel Barkley, and Mark Marshall, Legal Counsel to MTS. He expressed thanks to the members of the General Assembly Special Committee. Reverend Hill commended the Special Committee for its work and then an gave an overview of the decision-making process that led to the report and its recommendation.

Reverend Dr. Larry Blakeburn (Presbytery of East Tennessee) provided comments on the report of the General Assembly Special Committee. He expressed thanks to Reverend Hill and Reverend Rush as they worked cooperatively with the Special Committee. In addition, he acknowledged the contributions of the Reverend Michael Sharpe (Stated Clerk) and Mr. Jaime Jordan (Legal Counsel) to the Special Committee. Reverend Blakeburn noted that Cumberland Presbyterian theological education is not ended with the closing of MTS. He invited those participating in the meeting to think of ways to further that mission and to share those ideas with members of the Special Committee before the June 2026 meeting of the General Assembly in Rogers, Arkansas.

RECESS

The Moderator called at 2:17 p.m., the General Assembly back into session following a fifteen (15) minute recess.

RESUME BUSINESS FOR INFORMAL CONSIDERATION (QUESTIONS AND ANSWERS)

The Moderator called the General Assembly back from recess at 2:32 p.m. He invited the Reverend William (Rusty) Rustenhaven III (Trinity Presbytery) to serve as the facilitator for the question-and-answer session.

RECESS

The Moderator declared recess at 3:18 p.m. and to reconvene at 3:30 p.m.

GENERAL ASSEMBLY BUSINESS

At 3:32 p.m., the Moderator called the General Assembly back from recess.

REPORT OF MEMPHIS THEOLOGICAL SEMINARY BOARD OF TRUSTEES

The Moderator entertained a motion to adopt its recommendation, as the report has already been received. The motion was seconded and discussion followed.

The question was called.

Those participating on-line were invited to vote first. The Moderator reported no votes in favor of the recommendation and six in opposition. By voice vote of those in-person participants, the majority were in opposition to the recommendation. The report's recommendation was denied.

REPORT OF THE GENERAL ASSEMBLY SPECIAL COMMITTEE

Reverend Larry Blakeburn moved that that the recommendations of the General Assembly Special Committee be adopted. The motion was seconded and discussion followed.

Recommendations 1, 3, 4 and 5

The Moderator directed that a vote would be taken to adopt or deny recommendations, 1, 3, 4 and 5. He asked that those online be polled first. Seven votes on-line were cast in favor of adopting recommendations 1, 3, 4 and 5, and there were none against. The Moderator then polled those in-person and by voice vote the recommendations were adopted with none voting in opposition.

Recommendation 2

A motion made to amend the recommendation, to read as follows: "…and help to promote and support theological education for ministers and lay leaders; and to report on its progress to the 195th General Assembly."

Second received. Discussion followed.

The question was called amending Recommendation 2,

The Moderator polled those on-line with six in favor of the amendment and none opposed. The Moderator then polled those in-person. By voice vote the amendment was adopted. with none in opposition. The amendment passed.

The Moderator polled those on-line with five in favor of adopting Recommendation 2 as amended. The Moderator asked those in person to adopt Recommendation 2, as amended. By voice vote, with none in opposition, Recommendation 2 as amended was adopted.

The report was received and its recommendations adopted.

RECESS

At 4:01 p.m., the Moderator declared a ten-minute recess.

GENERAL ASSEMBLY BUSINESS RESUMES

At 4:11 p.m. the Moderator, Reverend Jhony Montaño called the General Assembly back into session.

READING OF THE MINUTES

The Reverend Lisa A. Scott, Engrossing Clerk, read the meeting minutes. The following corrections were received from the Commissioners. The Moderator entertained a motion to approve the minutes as read. A second was received. The Moderator asked that those on-line vote first, six were in favor of approving the minutes. On voice vote of those in person the minutes were approved we pith none in opposition.

CLOSING WORSHIP

Reverend Jen Newell led the closing worship with unison reading of Colossians 1:15-18. Reverend Mike Sharpe accompanied the congregation on the piano as it sang "We Are God's People." The Reverend Jhony Montaño shared a devotional. His text was 1 Corinthians 10:31 and his message, "Whatever you do, do it all for the glory of God." He invited three to offer a prayer based on the devotional.

ADJOURNMENT

The Moderator entertained a motion to adjourn and it was seconded. Reverend Jen Newell invited Reverend Dr. Blakeburn to pray for those present representing MTS and the Board of Trustee. The Commissioners and visitors gathered for prayer. Following the prayer, Reverend Newell gave the benediction.

The General Assembly adjourned at 4:45 p.m.

APPENDICES

THE CALL

THE CUMBERLAND PRESBYTERIAN CHURCH

OFFICE OF THE GENERAL ASSEMBLY

Michael G. Sharpe, Stated Clerk
msharpe@cumberland.org

Elizabeth A. Vaughn, Assistant to the Stated Clerk
eav@cumberland.org

To: Moderator Rev. Jhony Montaño

The undersigned members of the 194th General Assembly respectfully request that you call a meeting of the General Assembly to meet at the Brenthaven Cumberland Presbyterian Church, Brentwood, Tennessee (in the Nashville area) beginning at 1:00 pm on January 23, 2026, and continuing January 24, as necessary for the following purpose:

To hear relevant reports and take appropriate actions with respect to Memphis Theological Seminary of the Cumberland Presbyterian Church and theological education.

A General Assembly Special Committee was appointed by the 194th General Assembly to work in conjunction with Memphis Theological Seminary in Merger, Affiliation, and Partnership discussions, to review and evaluate all options and determine future needs for Clergy/Leadership Training in the denomination, in consultation with the General Assembly Corporation, the Pastoral Development Ministry Team, and the Program of Alternate Studies.

The Special Committee has determined that a called meeting is necessary to address urgent matters related to its assignment.

Signed:

Ministers	Presbytery	Elders	Presbytery
Larry Blakeburn	East Tennessee	Mo Ottinger	Robert Donnell
Kip Rush	Nashville	Guin Tyus	Nashville
Bobby Coeman	Arkansas	Brenda Howell	ColumbiaDavid
Linski	Grace	Donna Jo Thompson	Trinity
Lisa Oliver	Murfreesboro	Mike Salyer	Nashville
Michael Qualls	Midsouth	Sandra Smith	Red River
Bill James	Cornerstone	Dale Johnson	Hope
William Rustenhaven III	Trinity	Elizabeth Mills	Nashville
John Butler	Cumberland	Tim McDonald	Murfreesboro
Jason Mikel	Nashville	Tony Bird	East Tennessee

In response to the above request I hereby call the General Assembly to meet as above, at the hour, dates and place as set out for the purposes herein specified.

Signed: Jhony Montaño, General Assembly Moderator

I attest that this is a true and accurate statement of the call.

Signed: Michael Sharpe, General Assembly Stated Clerk

8207 Traditional Place, Cordova, TN 38016
(443)699-2321
Fax (901) 272-3913

NOTES

NOTES

NOTES

NOTES

NOTES

NOTES

NOTES